Gardener's Guide to the Pumpkin and Winter Squash

Growing, Harvesting and Storing Pumpkins and Winter Squash

Gardener's Guide to Growing Your Vegetable Garden – Book XIII

Paul R. Wonning

Gardener's Guide to the Pumpkin and Winter Squash

Published By Paul R. Wonning

Print Edition

paulwonning@gmail.com

If you would like email notification of when new Mossy Feet books become available email the author for inclusion in the subscription list.

Mossy Feet Books
www.mossyfeetbooks.com

Indiana Places

http://indianaplaces.blogspot.com/

Description

Gardener's Guide to the Pumpkin and Winter Squash includes instructions on growing, harvesting and storing pumpkins and winter squash. In addition to the fruit, both the flowers and the seed are edible. Gardeners will also find instructions for preparing tasty snacks from the squash, the blossoms and seeds. Pumpkins and other winter squash are a nutritious food source that the gardener can easily grow in their vegetable garden. Gardeners will find that the *Gardener's Guide to the Pumpkin and Winter Squash* is a valuable resource for their library.

Table of Contents

Gardener's Guide to the Pumpkin and Winter Squash

Paul R. Wonning

Introduction

Used by most people as a colorful autumn display, pumpkins and other winter squash can also provide a tasty, nutritious food source. Valued by the original Amerindian inhabitants of North and Central America, and the early European settlers, the winter squash will store for months. Used for pies, soup, baked dishes or roasted, the winter squash served as a main crop for many pioneer families. Roasted squash seeds also provide a tasty nutritious snack as well. Squash are easy to grow, but do require a fairly long growing season. Most also require a lot of space, however some are compact growers that even the smallest gardens can accommodate.

Common Name:

Pumpkin

The name "pumpkin," originally derives from the Greek word pepon, or "large melon," which translates as something large and round. The French converted this word to pompon, which the British translated as pumpion. This word evolved into its American name, pumpkin.

Botanical Name:

Cucurbita pepo

The cucurbita genus includes the summer squashes like zucchini, winter squashes like pumpkin and the ornamental gourds. The name derives from the Latin name for cucumber, a member of the same family.

Pepo derives from the Latin word meaning "large melon."

Family:

Cucurbitaceae - Cucumber

Cucurbitaceae

Sometimes called the cucumber, or gourd, family, this economically important family includes the genera Cucurbita (squash), Lagenaria (gourds), Citrullus (watermelon), and Cucumis (cucumber).

The family contains ninety-eight genera and 975 species. These genera's natural habits are mostly in the tropical regions and all are frost sensitive. Most of the species are annual vines with tendrils perpendicular to the leaf nodes The stem is hairy. The plants possess large, yellow or white uni-sexual flowers. The species either have male and female flowers on different plants (dioecious) or on the same plant (monoecious). The female flowers develop into a modified berry called a pepo. Most species have palmate, simple or lobed leaves.

Sun:

Full Sun

The pumpkin will require full sun, but can tolerate some light shade. If the site is shaded at all, the size and yield of the pumpkins will diminish. Afternoon sun is best.

Soil:

Pumpkins require fertile, well-drained soil with a ph between 6 and 6.5. Pumpkins cannot tolerate wet, soggy soils. A rich loam or sandy soil enriched with well-rotted compost or rotted manure is best.

Propagation:

Pumpkins are only propagated by seed.

Plant Height, Spread, Spacing:

Plant Height:

The plants will grow from eighteen to twenty-four inches tall.

Spread:

The spread depends upon the variety grown. Sprawling types can spread six to ten feet or more. Bush types will spread about three to five feet.

Spacing:

To grow well, sprawling types need about sixty square feet of space. Plant four or five seeds to a hill and space the hills about five feet apart in the row. Rows should be ten to twelve feet apart. Bush types can have the hills four or five feet apart with about six feet between the rows.

Flower Color, Description and Fragrance:

Pumpkin and winter squash, like all cucurbits, have two types of flowers, a male flower and a female flower. Both are funnel shaped and yellow. The male flower is much smaller that the female flower. Male flowers usually develop first, followed by the female flowers. The female will develop on a small, emerging fruit. After pollination, the blossom falls away and the fruit grows in size. Both the male and the female flowers are edible.

Pollination:

The plant has both male and female flowers on the same plant. Bees, bumble or honey bees, must visit first the male flower, then the female flower to pollinate it. Pollination is necessary for fruit to develop. If pollinating insects are in short supply, it is possible to hand pollinate the plants. Remove the male flower and rub the stamens on the anthers at the center of the plant. Most times hand pollination is not necessary.

Origins and History:

The Europeans learned to grow squash from the Amerindian tribes that inhabited North America at the time of settlement. The Italians developed the zucchini squash varieties in the late Nineteenth Century, probably near Milan. English colonists developed the pumpkin pie by cutting the top of the pumpkin off, removing the seeds and filling the interior with milk, spices and honey. They would then bake the pumpkin in hot coals.

Plant Description:

Pumpkin plants are sprawling vines with large, alternate, palm shaped leaves. The vine can grow eight to ten feet or more. Bush varieties do not vine, remaining compact.

Hardiness Zone:

Pumpkin and other squash are not hardy and do best in temperatures over seventy degrees.

Planting Seeds:

Most gardeners direct seed the seeds into ground that has been prepared well in advance after the last chance of frost has passed. Soil temperatures should be seventy degrees with a minimum of sixty degrees. Gardeners may plant the seeds in containers in the greenhouse or hot bed. Since they do not like to have their roots disturbed, plant in a pot no smaller than three inches about two to three weeks before the last expected frost.

Growing Seedlings:

Keep seedlings in pots well watered and expose to enough sunlight that they do not stretch. Garden grown seedlings need adequate water to ensure good growth. Do not over water or the seedlings can succumb to damping off or other fungal diseases. Transplant pots after the first true leaves form, after all danger of frost has passed.

Garden Culture and Uses:

To hasten harvest, use a black plastic mulch to warm the soil. Apply the mulch before direct seeding or transplanting. Use organic mulches instead of black plastic to stifle weeds and conserve moisture. Be aware that mulches of any kind may increase the slug population. Use diatomaceous earth or slug traps to deter them. Make sure to remove all crop residues at the end of the season to remove shelter for garden pests like squash bugs. Do not plant cucurbits like squash, melons and cucumbers in the same plot for two to three years to avoid fungal and bacterial infestations. Supply about one inch of water each week during the flowering season. The most important time for moisture is during bud and fruit development. Prepare the bed before planting with well-rotted compost. Use organic fertilizers like seaweed extract or fish emulsion to side dress growing crops. Spray directly on the foliage. Use of too much nitrogen may diminish the yield. It is best to irrigate with a soaker hose. If using a sprinkling can, try to avoid watering the leaves as that can lead to fungal diseases.

Growing the Big Ones

Planting the pumpkins in fertile soil will result in a crop of nice pumpkins. Many gardeners are interested in growing big pumpkins, while some competitive growers want to grow gigantic ones of several hundred pounds for pumpkin growing contests. If really big pumpkins are part of your plan, then you must take extra steps to grow the enormous ones. First is sunlight. The pumpkins will need eight to ten hours of uninterrupted sunlight. Pumpkins require a high degree of soil fertility to yield pumpkins. To grow the big ones, the gardener needs to supplement the vines with several timed feedings during the course of the season. Fertilize the beds at planting with plenty of well-rotted compost or manure. If using poultry manure, be careful, as this manure is "hot" and can burn plants with excess nitrogen. Make sure it is well rotted. When the plants are about a foot long, start feeding them with a high nitrogen fertilizer. Just before bloom, switch to a high phosphorus feed. If gigantic fruit are the goal, thin the vines to just two or three pumpkins per vine and pinch off new vine growth after a few pumpkins have formed. This will focus the plants energy on those few pumpkins. Feed at regular intervals; say once a week or so. Place a board or sturdy cardboard under the pumpkins when small, allowing you to turn them as they grow. This helps the pumpkin become even in shape. Be patient. Prize winning pumpkin growers spend years perfecting their craft, and many have "secret" methods that they guard carefully.

Problems:

Squash bug

Handpick the insects, placing them in a jar or other container with a tight fitting lid for disposal. Bury or compost plant residues after harvest, as the adults can over winter in crop debris.

Squash vine borer

Remove the borers by hand and destroy them.

Spotted Cucumber Beetles

Cucumber beetles emerge from dormancy in spring before the weather is warm enough for cucumbers or zucchini to begin growing. When zucchini starts growing, cucumber beetles will begin feeding on leaves and fruits. The spotted beetles are little yellow insects about a half-inch long, with black spots. Trap them with yellow sticky traps or cover the plants with a floating row cover, like spun bond fiber. Be sure to remove the cover when flowers appear so the bees can pollinate the flowers. .

Striped Cucumber Beetles

These insects are similar to the cucumber beetle in size and shape, except they have black and yellow stripes. Controls are similar to the cucumber beetle.

Squash Vine Borers

Squash vine borers are the larvae of wasp-like moths. The borers bore into zucchini stems and eat their way through them. Look for sawdust-like excrement near small holes to know they are present. The plants will suddenly wilt and may die. Slit the damaged vine with a sharp knife and remove the borers with a tweezers. Cover the damaged section with well-aged compost and the plant will continue growth. Alternatively, spray the base of stems once a week with Bacillus thuringiensis.

Blossom-End Rot

Irregular watering and soil calcium deficiency can result in poor water uptake into the plant. This may result in the blossom end of the fruit to become leathery and sunken on the end of the developing fruit. This is called blossom-end rot. Use ground oyster shells or a calcium-rich fertilizer to counter blossom-end rot and water consistently.

Powdery Mildew

Watering using a sprinkler can cause the zucchini plants to develop powdery mildew. This is a fungus disease caused by too wet conditions. Use a fungicide to control. Sulfur is an organic control.

Aphids, White Flies and Spider Mites

Common pests associated with summer squash are aphids, spider mites, squash vine borers, and whiteflies. The appearance of fine, spider webs around the leaves of the plants is a sign of spider mites. The mites are tiny spiders that can kill the plants. Aphids appear on the leaves undersides most of the time. They will puncture leaves and stems, sucking out the plant juices. White flies are small, white flies that fly around the plant when disturbed. Like aphids and mites, they will suck the juices from the plants, weakening and eventually killing them. All three insects can also carry diseases and infest other areas of the garden. Use insecticidal soap to control aphids, spider mites, and whiteflies. Be sure to dilute the spray and refrain from spraying in the heat of the day because squash leaves may burn easily. It is wise to test a few leaves first before spraying the entire plant. Do not forget the undersides of leaves, where spider mites and whiteflies usually hide.

Diseases

Common diseases include bacterial wilt, downy mildew, powdery mildew, and viruses. In the case of bacterial wilt, leaves begin to die. Cut the wilted stem and touch the tip of your knife to the sap. If it is milky and sticky, your plant is infected. Destroy infected plants immediately. Bacterial wilt, mildews and most viruses can be controlled or prevented with good cultural practices. Inspect plants often and control insect pests that can spread disease. Keep the garden clean and free of weeds and debris. Reduce the likelihood of mildews proper watering and good air circulation. Once the plant contracts most of these diseases, they will likely not recover. Remove and discard. Do not throw in the compost heap, as that can spread the disease.

Medicinal uses:

The author does not recommend nor endorse use of pumpkin as a medicine. This section is for informational uses only. If you want to use this as an herb or for medical uses it is best to consult with a physician or health care provider before doing so.

The rind of the pumpkin and the leaves contain proteins that have antibiotic and anti-fungal properties. Pumpkin seeds can relieve tapeworm infestations and inhibit kidney stone formation. Pumpkin is high in vitamin C and carotene, both of which have proven beneficial. A diet that incorporates pumpkin regularly can help eye health, prevent obesity, prevent diabetes, and help maintain healthy blood pressure. The beta-carotene in pumpkins has also been shown to help prevent colon and other types of cancer. Consuming pumpkin can increase a woman's fertility, while the Vitamin A in pumpkin can help stimulate lactation.

Food Uses:

Most of these uses involve pumpkin; however, any winter squash will work.

Puree

Most people make puree from the pumpkin's flesh. To make puree, cut the pumpkin in half, scoop out the seeds and guts. Save both of these, as both have uses. After cleaning the inside of the pumpkin, cut into smaller pieces and roast in the oven until the flesh is tender, usually around forty-five minutes to an hour. Peel the pumpkin flesh, discarding the skin. Place the pulp into a blender, food processor or food mill and process until smooth. The puree is useful to make pies, pumpkin butter and other tasty dishes. The puree may be frozen or canned for later use. To freeze, just fill freezer containers with the puree and put in the freezer.

Soups Stock

The stringy insides of the pumpkin make a tasty stock for soups and stews. Place in a saucepan filled with water and add other vegetables like celery, carrots, etc. boil for about thirty minutes. Compost the vegetables and use or freeze the stock for soups and stews.

Pumpkin Seeds

Pumpkin seeds are a great, nutritious snack. To make, clean the seeds well and boil them for about ten minutes. Coat the boiled seeds with vegetable oil and spread out on a baking sheet. Bake the seeds for about thirty minutes at about 110 degrees. Flavor them with salt, paprika or your favorite seasoning.

Grate the raw flesh to use in pumpkin cakes and breads.

Baking Pumpkin and Winter Squash

Baking the pumpkin whole is a quick and easy way to enjoy pumpkin. Use a small pumpkin, cut the top off as if you are making a jack o' lantern. Save the lid. Scoop out the insides, saving the seeds for roasting, if desired. Heat enough cream to fill the pumpkin and add some seasonings like garlic, thyme and cloves. There are tons of recipes on the internet for this. Fill the pumpkin with the hot, seasoned cream, and put the lid on. Bake for about ninety minutes at 400 degrees. Scoop out the flesh into bowls and serve.

Roasting

To roast pumpkin or any other winter squash, cut the fruit into small pieces, about two inches square, more or less. Cut the peel away and place in a plastic bowl with a tight fitting lid. Add a bit of vegetable oil, onion powder, garlic power (or your favorite seasoning) and put on the lid. Shake until the pieces are coated with the oil and seasonings, then place on a baking tray. Put in a pre-heated oven and roast at 400 degrees for thirty to forty-five minutes. The flesh should be soft with a crusty brown covering. Serve the roasted wedged or freeze them for later use.

Fresh Blossoms

The blossoms are also edible. The female blossoms are best battered and deep-fried. Stuff them and bake them or use fresh as a garnish.

Harvesting:

Harvested properly, pumpkins and other winter squash can keep for months in storage. This keeping quality is one of the reasons they were such a valuable food resource for the Amerindians and pioneers. Once the skin has hardened and the color has developed completely, the squash is ready for harvest. If in doubt, press a fingernail against the skin of the squash. If it leaves a mark, the squash is still not completely mature. Squash take many months to mature. Sometimes an early frost may threaten the squash. If a hard frost threatens, cover the squash vines with blankets. Do not use plastic, as frost can still form under it. If long-term storage is a goal for your pumpkins, cut the ripened squash from the vine with a sharp knife. Pulling the fruit from the vine, or using the stem as a handle to carry the squash can result in the stem separating from the fruit. This creates an opening into the squash for bacteria, which can spoil the squash. Do not wash freshly harvested pumpkins. Store them for a week or so in a warm, sunny spot for several days. Do not damage the skins, as any cuts, scrapes or other damage can allow bacteria to spoil the squash.

Storage:

Gardeners may leave the winter squash in the garden to cure during the first, light frosts. If the temperature threatens to drop below 27 - 30 degrees, remove the fruits to avoid loss. Wash the fruits with a mild bleach solution, two tablespoons of bleach to a gallon of water, and allow them to dry. Commercial growers cure the fruits at 80 - 85 degrees for a week. This may be impractical for the gardener, but curing in the house or other area of warm temperatures for a few days can be beneficial. To store long term, place the squash in a dark area between 50 - 60 degrees. Store them on a porous surface like hay, cardboard or wooden shelves. Storage on a stone or concrete floor can lead to rot. Under ideal conditions, winter squash can last three to six months in storage. Inspect the stored squash occasionally for rotting fruits. Remove any that have spoiled and wipe any that touched them with a mild bleach solution.

Winter Squash Cultivars:

Acorn Squash

Butternut Squash

Buttercup Squash

Cushaws

Delicata Squash

Hubbard Squash

Kabocha Squash

Pumpkins

Blue Hokkaido Pumpkin

Cheese Pumpkins

Red Kuri Pumpkins

Rouge Vif d'Etampes Pumpkins

Sugar Pie Pumpkins

White Pumpkins

Spaghetti Squash

Sweet Dumpling Squash

Turban Squash

Acorn Squash

This acorn shaped squash has pumpkin like ridges. Most varieties have a dark green skin and feature yellow flesh, though different colors have been developed. Acorn squash may be baked, steamed, sautéed or stuffed with rice, meat and other ingredients. Most of these squash will be from two to five pounds in weight.

Varieties include:

Heirloom Table Queen - 85 Days

Festival Hybrid - 100 Days

Early Acorn Hybrid - 75 Days

Table Ace - 75 Days

Ebony - 80 Days

Cream of the Crop - 80 Days

Butternut Squash

This squash is the most common one grown in home gardens because of its ease of growing and productive vines. Butternut squash is an elongated, dumbbell shaped squash that usually has a tan color. The one to two pound squash keep for months properly stored and are excellent roasted, stuffed and to stuff ravioli. The moist, yellow flesh tastes best after a month or two in storage. The skin is edible, making peeling unnecessary. The productive, firm vines resist squash borers.

Butter Boy Hybrid - 80 Days

Waltham Butternut - 85 Days

Autumn Glow - 80 Days

Argonaut Hybrid - 140 Days

Buttercup Squash

Buttercup squash are usually dark green, pumpkin shaped with a dry, yellow sweet flesh great for roasting, soups and stews. The squash will average from three to five pounds and have excellent storage qualities. The squash will keep up to nine months in storage and will have the best taste after about two to four months of storage.

'Bonbon' Buttercup (F1 hybrid, 95 days)

'Burgess Buttercup' (Heirloom, Open Pollinated, 90-95 days)

'Winter Sweet' (F1 Hybrid, 95 days)

'Cha Cha' (F1 Hybrid, 90-95 days)

'Shokichi Shiro' (F1 Hybrid, 100 days)

'Discus Bush Buttercup' (Open Pollinated, 90 days)

Cushaws

Also called the Tennessee sweet potato and the cushaw pumpkin, this green striped crook necked squash grows from ten to twenty inches in length, ten inches in diameter and weights from ten to twenty pounds. Biologists believe that the cushaw originated between 3000 and 7000 BC in Mesoamerica. Resistant to squash vine borer, cushaws have similar food uses to other squash. The cushaw is popular in Caribbean recipes and is grown extensively in the south. It can tolerate hot, humid conditions and low rainfall.

Albino

Hopi

Albine

Pepita

Australian,

Cochiti Puebla

Gila

Gila Cliff Dweller

Gold Striped

Green Striped

Hopi

Hopi Black Green

Longneck

Magdalena Striped

Neckless

Old Fashioned

Papalote Ranch

Parral

Pure White

Santa Domingo

Solid Green

Tri-Color

White

White Crookneck or White Honathan

Winter

Delicata Squash

Also known as peanut squash, Bohemian squash, or sweet potato squash, these cucumber shaped squash are cream colored with a green stripe. The squash have a delicate, edible skin with a reputation of being easy to cook. The flesh has a creamy flavor and texture that cooks steam, bake, sauté or microwave. These squash do not keep as well as other winter squash, but they can be frozen. Most varieties mature in around eighty to one hundred days. Most Delicata squash grow as vines, but plant breeders have developed bush varieties.

Bush Delicata

Sugar Loaf

Honey Boat

Hubbard Squash

This pear shaped, "warty" skinned squash weighs from eight to twenty pounds and has a sweet flesh best used for pies, purees and mashes. This squash should keep for six months in a dry, cool environment. The skin is extremely hard and the squash can be hard to peel. Many cooks cut the squash into sections, roast the squash with the skin on, flesh side down and then scrape the flesh from the skin. Use the cooked flesh mixed with wild rice in a casserole, in soups and stews or just enjoy as a roasted treat. The raw pieces will keep up to five days in the refrigerator if wrapped in plastic.

Blue Hubbard

Golden Hubbard

True Green

Boston Marrow

Sweet Fall

Chicago Warted

Kabocha Squash

Also called Japanese pumpkin, Kabocha is a pumpkin shaped Asian squash with knobby skin. The green color is punctuated with cream stripes. The squash range from two to six pounds with the heaviest reaching eight pounds. The peel is edible and the flesh has a consistency between sweet potatoes and pumpkin. Some varieties taste like a Russet potato and many cooks substitute it for potatoes in recipes.

Ajihei

Ajihei No. 107

Ajihei No. 331

Ajihei No. 335

Cutie

Ebisu

Emiguri

Miyako

Pumpkins

The pumpkin is the most popular of the winter squashes. The orange to deep yellow skinned squash has thin ribs, thick yellow flesh and keeps well in winter storage. Gardeners will find a wide selection of cultivars that range from small fruits of a pound or so to behemoths that can grow to several hundred pounds. Pumpkins may be roasted, put into soups and stews, baked, stuffed, and made into pie. Below is a partial listing of the dozens of varieties of pumpkins available for gardeners to grow.

Small varieties

All 2 to 5 pounds, 100 to 110 days to harvest

Baby Bear

Baby Pam

Small Sugar

Spooktacular

Sugar Treat

Winter Luxury

Intermediate varieties

All 8 to 15 pounds, 100 to 110 days to harvest

Autumn Gold

Bushkin

Frosty

Funny Face

Harvest Moon

Jack-o-Lantern

Long Island Cheese

Lumina (white skin)

Spirit

Young's Beauty

Large varieties

All 15 to 40 pounds, 100 to 110 days to harvest

Aspen

Big Autumn

Big Tom

Connecticut Field

Ghost Rider

Happy Jack

Hercules/Super Herc/HMX 3692 PMR

Howden Field

Jackpot

Jumpin' Jack

Magic Lantern PMR

Pankow's Field

Jumbo varieties

All 50 to 100 pounds, or much more; 120 days to harvest

Atlantic Giant

Big Max

Big Moon

Mammoth Gold

Prizewinner

Hokkaido Pumpkin

The Japanese developed the Hokkaido pumpkin from New England pumpkins. The teardrop shaped pumpkins range from four to twelve pounds and feature a smooth, dry, sweet golden flesh. The skin is edible. Use Hokkaido for soups, sauces, jams, pies, stuffing, in risottos or in baked dishes, as a grilled dish or side dish in different variations. This squash should keep for six months in a dry basement.

Red Kuri

Blue Hokkaido

Potimarron

Long Island Cheese Pumpkins

An old variety that traces its origins to early Long Island colonists, the Long Island Cheese Pumpkin is has the oval shape of a loaf of farmhouse cheese. The pale orange squash has medium ridges. The Long Island Cheese Pumpkin ranges from six to ten pounds. Each plant should produce two of the medium sized, flattened pumpkins with superior keeping abilities. The deep orange flesh is excellent for use in all pumpkin recipes.

Rouge Vif d'Etampes Pumpkins

This old, French heirloom pumpkin matures in about 95 days. The pumpkins resemble Cheese Pumpkins in shape, but have an attractive deep orange skin. The name derives from French and means "vivid red." The pumpkins make an excellent fall display. Gardeners may pick these squash during the summer to use like a summer squash, or leave them on the vine to mature in the fall. A good yielder, the pumpkin's moderately sweet flesh is good for pies. The pumpkins should average ten to fifteen pounds at maturity.

Sugar Pie Pumpkins

These small pumpkins are around six to seven inches in diameter and average five to six pounds. Sugar Pie Pumpkins have a sweet, firm flesh that will cook down to a smooth, consistent puree. The bright orange flesh is among the sweetest and flavorful of the pumpkins. Slice the pumpkins and roast or grill them. The Sugar Pie also is delicious baked, in pies, cheesecake, pancakes and flan. Hollow it out, stuff and bake it. This is an heirloom variety grown since colonial times.

White Pumpkins

Pumpkin growers have developed natural white pumpkins. These pumpkins are easier to carve, as the skin is thinner. The flesh is orange, like other pumpkin varieties and their culinary uses identical. Varieties include Lumina, Cotton Candy and miniature Baby Boo.

Spaghetti Squash

Spaghetti squash flesh cooks down to a stringy consistency that resembles spaghetti, hence its name. Each squash should produce between four and six four-pound squash. As with other squash, allow to mature before harvest, which should take place before frost. It will keep in the refrigerator about two weeks. Spaghetti squash should keep up to three months under cool, dry conditions. For long term, store in a dry, cool area. Ideal storage is between fifty to sixty degrees. Excess humidity will destroy the squash's texture. To prepare, cut the squash in half and remove the seeds from the inside. Coat the inside of the squash with olive oil, salt and pepper. Preheat an oven to 375 degrees. Place the squash halves upside down on a cookie sheet and bake until a fork will easily penetrate the skin, about forty minutes. Scrape out the spaghetti-like interior and prepare using your favorite pasta recipe.

Sweet Dumpling Squash

The diminutive sweet dumpling squash is small enough for a single serving. The four inch, one-pound squash has sweet, tender, orange flesh. The round, flat-topped squash has cream-colored skin with dark green splotches in the grooves. The medium length vines will yield about eight to ten squash each. It should mature in about 100 days.

Turban Squash

Known as Turk's Turban or French turban, the unique shape of this squash gives it its name. The multi-colored oval shaped lower part of the squash has a smaller "turban" on top. The color of the squash varies considerably from squash to squash, mostly consisting of orange, green, white, cream and yellow. This beautiful squash originated around 1820 and is considered an heirloom variety. They store well and have a nutty flavor.

USDA Nutrition Facts

Serving size: ½ cup (cubed, cooked winter squash - Amount Per Serving

Calories 40

Calories from Fat 0

% Daily Value*

Total Fat 0g - 0%

Saturated Fat 0g - 0%

Trans Fat - 0g

Cholesterol 0mg - 0%

Sodium 0mg - 2%

Total Carbohydrate - 9 g 3%

Dietary Fiber - 3g 12%

Sugars - 3g

Protein - 1g

Vitamin A - 110%

Vitamin C - 15%

Calcium - 2%

Iron - 2%

Seed Companies to Buy Pumpkin Seed:

Seed Available From:

This is not an all inclusive list. It includes most of the best catalog and online places to find squash seeds.

Seed Companies to Buy Lettuce Seed:

Burpee

W. Atlee Burpee Company

Warminster PA 18974

1-800-888-1447

www.burpee.com

The W. Atlee Burpee Company is one of the leading seed companies in the gardening industry. The catalog lists good selections of annual and perennial flowers as well as vegetable seeds. Many, many tomatoes listed in addition to sweet corn and squash.

Farmers Seed and Nursery

Division of Plantron, Inc

818 NW 4th Street

Fairbault, MN 55021

1-850-7334-1623

www.farmerseed.com

This catalog has a good selection of nursery stock including ornamental shrubs and trees. Fruit includes strawberries, blackberries and raspberries. Other types of fruit trees and vines, too. Nut trees, perennial plants and roses, also. There is a good selection of vegetable seed.

George W. Park Seed Company

1 Parkton Ave

Greenwood, SC 29647-0001

1-800-845-3369

www.parkseed.com

146 pages

This bountiful catalog has extensive offerings of all categories of seeds - herbs, vegetables, annual and perennial seeds. There is also a generous offering of fruit and berry plants like grapes, blackberries and strawberries.

Gurney's Seed and Nursery

PO Box 4178

Greendale, IN 47025-4178

513-354-1491

www.gurneys.com

Gurney's large format catalog offers large selections of vegetables, flowers, fruits and supplies for gardening. They also list trees, shrubs, roses, and nut trees.

Harris Seeds

355 Paul Road

PO Box 24966

Rochester, NY 14624-0966

1-800-514-4441

www.harrisseeds.com

Heavy selection of vegetable seeds, with a nice offering of flower seeds, too. They have almost 20 pages of gardening supplies like seed starting equipment, flats and carts.

John Scheepers Kitchen Garden Seeds

23 Tulip Drive

PO Box 838

Bantam, CT 06750-0638

1-860-567-6086

www.kitchengardenseeds.com

This catalog focuses on vegetables and herbs. It has unusual and old time varieties as well as some of the favorites. The salad green selection of seeds is excellent. There are also Asian greens and sprouting seeds. There are some flower seeds, mostly annual fragrant and cutting flowers. This is a nice catalog with some unusual seed offerings.

Johnny's Selected Seeds

955 Benton Ave.

Winslow, ME 04901

Phone: 877-564-6697

Fax: 800-738-6314

Annuals

Bulbs

Perennials

Flower, Vegetable and Wildflower Seeds

Fruit Trees and Berries

Garden Supplies, Tools and Power Equipment

Gifts and Decorative Accessories

Greenhouses and Indoor Gardening Supplies

Ground Covers, Shrubs, Trees, and Vines

Herbs and Vegetables

Irrigation Supplies and Equipment

Fertilizer, Weed & Pest Control Products

Magazines and Books

Ornamental Grasses and Plants

Website: Johnnyseeds.com

homegarden@johnnyseeds.com

J. W. Jung Seed Company

335 South High Street

Randolph, WI 53957-0001

1-800-247-5864

www.jungseed.com

Jung sells a very interesting mix of fruit trees and plants, shrubs and trees, vegetable and flower seed, and gardening supplies. Perennial plants, flower bulbs, lilies and roses are included in the offerings. This is a "must have" catalog for the gardener.

Pinetree Garden Seeds

PO Box 300

New Gloucester, ME 04260

1-926-3400

www.superseeds.com

The catalog claims over 900 varieties of seeds, bulbs, tubers, garden books

and products. The listings are extensive with the emphasis on vegetable seeds. There are sections for ethnic vegetables like Asian, Italian, and Latin American. The flower offerings include both annual and perennialflower seeds.

of gardening related books.

Seeds of Change

PO Box 15700

Santa Fe NM 87592-1500

1-888-762-7333

www.seedsofchange.com

84 pages

This catalog is for vegetable lovers as it is mostly devoted to them, and all seeds sold by this company are certified organic. There is a section of flower seeds, but veggies take center stage. There is a full page of garlic varieties! Gourmet greens and herbs are in good supply, too.

There is also a good selection of gardening books and gardening supplies.

Select Seeds

180 Stickney Hill Road

Union, CT 06076

1-860-684-9310

www.selectseeds.com

If you are looking for something a bit out of the mainstream or "different" then Select Seeds is the catalog you are looking for. Most of the seeds and plants offered are not found in the major outlets. Special sections for fragrant and old fashioned plants are featured. This catalog is a must for the home gardener looking for a flower garden that stands out a bit.

Seymours Selected Seeds

334 West Stroud Street

Randolph, WI 53596

1-800-353-9516

www.seymourseedusa.com

This small catalog is packed with a full selection of annual and perennial flowers for the home gardner. Many unusual varieties and old time favorites. There is also a nice selection of bulbs and perennial plants.

Southern Exposure Seed Exchange

PO Box 460

Mineral, VA 23117

Phone: 540-894-9480

Fax: 540-894-9481

Annuals

Bulbs

Perennials

Exotic Plants and Flowers

Flower, Vegetable and Wildflower Seeds

Fruit Trees and Berries

Garden Supplies, Tools and Power Equipment

Gifts and Decorative Accessories

Ground Covers, Shrubs, Trees, and Vines

Herbs and Vegetables

Irrigation Supplies and Equipment

Fertilizer, Weed & Pest Control Products

Magazines and Books

Ornamental Grasses and Plants

Other

Southern Exposure Seed Exchange is a source for vegetables selected in a day where taste and local adaptability were the primary factors. They have an extensive line of heirloom and other open pollinated seeds and seed saving supplies. Many varieties are certified organic. They also company a wide variety of garlic and perennial onion bulbs and medicinal herb rootstock. We are a source for naturally colored cotton seeds.

www.southernexposure.com

Email Contact: gardens@southernexposure.com

Swallowtail Garden Seeds

122 Calistoga Road, #178

Santa Rosa, CA 95409

Phone: Toll Free 1-877-489-7333

707-538-3585

http://www.swallowtailgardenseeds.com/

Territorial Seed Company

PO Box 158

Cottate Grove, OR 97424

1-541-942-9547

www.territorialseed.com

This is a good catalog for market gardeners. Territorial has a big selection of vegetables. There are a lot of different varieties of beans, with 25 pound bags available many varieties. Sweet and popcorn are also well represented. Many varieties of lettuce also listed. Melons, peppers, peas, pumpkins and squash, along with boatloads of tomatoes. They also have a large selecion of annual flowers, available in larger quantities,

so small greenhouse growers would find this catalog helpful. There are approximately 30 varieties of sunflowers, and lots of herbs. There is a good selection of growing supplies, including several types of spun bond fabric row covers. You will find a pretty good selection of

organic growing aids in here also.Also a small selection of honey bee

supplies, including a mason bee starter kit.

Thompson and Morgan

220 Faraday Ave

Jackson NJ 08527

1-800-274-7333

www.thompsonandmorgan.com

200 pages of pure joy! Thompson and Morgan is one of the most complete seed catalogs available to the home gardener. You will find something of everything including the most popular annual and perennial flowers, vegetables and herbs, tree seeds and houseplants. There are hard to find varieties, standard varieties and some downright odd and unusual varieties.

This catalog focuses on seeds, so you won't find many gardening supplies.

Thompson and Morgan is one seed catalog the serious gardener shouldn't be without.

Totally Tomatoes

334 West Stroud Street

Randolph, WI 53956

1-800-345-5977

www.totallytomato.com

41 pages of nothing but tomatoes. They have the standard varieties available everywhere like Burpee Big Boy and Park Whopper. But there are many hard to find varieties like Aunt Ruby's German Green, Dixie Golden Giant and Bloody Butcher. They also have a good selection of peppers .

Urban Farmer Seeds

4105 Indiana 32 West

Westfield, IN 46074

1-317-600-2807

customerservice@ufseeds.com

http://www.ufseeds.com/

Vermont Bean Seed Company

334 W Stroud Street

Randolph, WI 53956

800-349-1071

www.vermontbean.com

These folks really do have the beans, sixteen pages of them. The catalog is chuck full of other stuff, too. Vegetable seeds are in good supply as well as some flower seeds and herbs. They also sell vegetable and flower plants.

Garden supplies include a nice selection of organic garden aids,and seed starting supplies.

Acknowledgments

http://motherhood.modernmom.com/cushaw-squash-varieties-14381.html

http://www.gardeningknowhow.com/edible/vegetables/squash/delicata-squash-information.htm

https://en.wikipedia.org/wiki/Delicata_squash

http://www.almanac.com/plant/pumpkins

https://en.wikipedia.org/wiki/Pumpkin

http://www.gardening-advice.net/growing-pumpkins.html

http://homeguides.sfgate.com/pumpkin-soil-needs-29785.html

http://www.hortmag.com/plants/tips-for-growing-pumpkins

https://extension.illinois.edu/pumpkins/history.cfm

http://www.gardeningknowhow.com/edible/vegetables/pumpkin/post-harvest-pumpkin-storage.htm

https://extension.illinois.edu/hortihints/0410c.html

http://www.grow-it-organically.com/winter-squash-varieties.html

http://www.backyard-vegetable-gardening.com/acorn-squash-varieties.html

http://www.thekitchn.com/the-11-varieties-of-winter-squash-you-need-to-know-ingredient-intelligence-157857

https://www.google.com/url?sa=t&rct=j&q=&esrc=s&source=web&cd=4&cad=rja&uact=8&ved=0ahUKEwj5jPW2mpbOAhWGYiYKHcWWBeMQFghFMAM&url=http%3A%2F%2Flocalfoods.about.com%2Fod%2Fwintersquashpumpkin%2Fss%2FTypes-Of-Winter-Squash.htm&usg=AFQjCNER-3t_Y-Kzq_JPfedyEDHfZbhp9Q&sig2=AbZZ0UlV697xHkGBFhb0Zw

http://www.gardeningknowhow.com/edible/vegetables/squash/growing-cushaw-squash-plants.htm

http://www.bbcgoodfood.com/howto/guide/how-cook-pumpkin

http://thepioneerwoman.com/cooking/make-your-own-pumpkin-puree/

http://earth911.com/food/10-uses-for-your-pumpkin/

http://www.food.com/recipe/spicy-roast-pumpkin-193241

http://www.emaxhealth.com/1506/61/34277/medicinal-qualities-pumpkin.html

http://www.medicalnewstoday.com/articles/279610.php

http://www.rodalesorganiclife.com/garden/how-pick-perfect-pumpkins-squash

http://www.sparkpeople.com/resource/perfect_prod_detail.asp?ppid=88

http://www.gardeningblog.net/how-to-grow/spaghetti-squash/

http://wgno.com/2014/10/27/whats-the-deal-with-white-pumpkins/

http://gonewengland.about.com/od/halloween/g/white-pumpkin.htm

http://www.specialtyproduce.com/produce/Organic_Sugar_Pie_Pumpkins_2566.php

http://www.johnnyseeds.com/p-7184-rouge-vif-detampes.aspx

http://www.rareseeds.com/rouge-vif-d-etampes-/

https://www.slowfoodusa.org/ark-item/long-island-cheese-pumpkin

http://www.hokkaidopumpkin.com

About the Author

Gardening, history and travel seem an odd soup in which to stew one's life, but Paul has done just that. A gardener since 1975, he has spent his spare time reading history and traveling with his wife. He gardens, plans his travels and writes his books out in the sticks near a small town in southeast Indiana. He enjoys sharing the things he has learned about gardening, history and travel with his readers. The many books Paul has written reflect that joy of sharing. He also writes fiction in his spare time. Read and enjoy his books, if you will. Or dare.

Now, back to writing, if he can get the cat off the keyboard.

Join Paul on Facebook
https://www.facebook.com/Mossy-Feet-Books-474924602565571/
Twitter
https://twitter.com/MossyFeetBooks
paulwonning@gmail.com

Mossy Feet Books Catalog

To Get Your Free Copy of the Mossy Feet Books Catalogue, Click This Link.

http://mossyfeetbooks.blogspot.com/

Gardening Books

Fantasy Books

Humor

Science Fiction

Semi - Autobiographical Books

Travel Books

Sample - Gardeners Guide to Growing Green Beans

Common Name:

Garden Bean, Snap bean, green bean, string bean

Snap bean refers to the "snap" sound the bean makes when cooks break the bean in half. Many call them string beans because of the "string" of skin that runs along the seam of the bean that resembles a thread when removed. Since people consume these beans unripe with the seed still in the pod, they call them "green beans." The author refers to them as a whole in this book as garden beans because both the green and dry versions of beans are included in this volume.

Botanical Name:

Phaseolus vulgaris

The genus name is the Greek name for a type of bean. Vulgaris is Latin for common.

Family:

Leguminosae, Fabaceae

Fabaceae is a new name fixed by botanists that derives from the Latin word "bean." Leguminosae is an older name, still used, which is a Latin term that refers to the fruit.

The Fabaceae family is a large family that consists of annual, perennial plants, trees, vines and herbs. It is the third largest plant family with 630 genera and over one8,860 species. Many of the members of this family have great economic importance. These include peas, beans, soybeans, licorice, alfalfa and clover. Most members of this family have a fruit that botanists refer to as a legume. This seeds develop inside a pod that has two seams. Several seeds usually inhabit each pod. Most members of this family also host bacteria called rhizobia in nodules on their roots. These bacteria have the important function of taking nitrogen from the air and converting it to a form that most plants can use. This trait makes legumes an important part of a gardeners plant rotation. These bacteria convert more nitrogen than their hosts can use. The remainder of the nitrogen stays in the soil after the plant has completed its life cycle, making it available to other plants.

Sun:

Full sun

At least six to eight hours of sun per day

Soil:

Rich, well drained slightly acidic pH of about 6.0 to 6.2. They dont need nitrogen fertilizer because they can fix their own from the atmosphere

Hardiness Zone:

Garden beans are tropical in origin and are quite sensitive to cold and frost. Plant them only after the soil has warmed and danger of frost has passed. Planting too early will result in rotted seeds, not early beans.

Origins:

Snap beans originated in the hot tropics, mostly Central and South America, Indian and China. Spanish conquistadores carried the garden bean to Europe in one597. The American Indians cultivated snap beans, growing them in the same mounds with corn and squash, the famed "three sisters" growing system. The Amerindians would not have eaten these beans green. Instead, they would have let them mature and harvested them as dry beans.

Propagation:

Seed

Plant snap beans in the garden after all danger of frost have past. They will take seven to ten days to germinate when the soil temperature has reached 65 - 70 degrees. Plant the seeds one and a half to two inches deep and about six inches apart in the row. Rows separation depends upon you gardening method. If you hand cultivate or grow in raised beds plant the seeds about six inches apart. If planting in rows, make sure the row width accommodates your garden tiller or other machine. Pole beans will need some sort of trellis system.

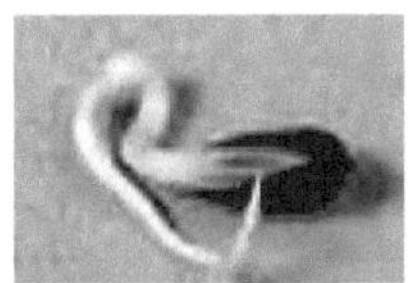

You can plant beans early in a hot bed or greenhouse. Plant them in a three inch pot three to four weeks before frost and set the seedlings in the garden after all danger of frost has passed. Use a big enough pot so you dont have to transplant the seedlings into a bigger one, as bean seedlings dont transplant well.

Plant Height, Spread, Spacing:

Plant Height:

Bush - Twelve to twenty four inches

Half Runner - Twenty to thirty six inches

Pole - Six to fifteen feet

Spread:

Bush - Twelve to fifteen inches

Half Runner - Twelve to fifteen inches

Pole - Twelve to fifteen inches

Spacing:

Bush - Two to six inches apart in rows twenty-four to thirty inches apart

Half Runner - Four to eight inches in rows twenty four to thirty six inches apart

Pole - Four to eight inches in rows twenty four to thirty six inches apart

Mossy Feet Books
www.mossyfeetbooks.com

Made in United States
Troutdale, OR
03/15/2025